Love, God & Relationships

Christine Emelone

Kingdom Publishers

www.kingdompublishers.co.uk

Love, God and Relationships

Copyright © Christine Marie Emelone

All rights reserved.

No part of this book may be reproduced in any form by photocopying or any electronic or mechanical means, including information storage or retrieval systems, without permission in writing from both the copyright owner and the publisher of the book. The right of Christine Marie Emelone to be identified as the author of this work has been asserted by him/her in accordance with the Copyright, Designs and Patents Act 1988 and any subsequent amendments thereto. A catalogue record for this book is available from the British Library.

ISBN: 978-1-913247-14-0

1st Edition by Kingdom Publishers
Kingdom Publishers
London, UK.

You can purchase copies of this book from any leading bookstore or email contact@kingdompublishers.co.uk

Contents

Chapter 1 - *What does a Christian relationship look like?*   8

Chapter 2 - *Your relationship with God*   13

Chapter 3 - *Why putting God first in your life and relationship is worth it*   18

Chapter 4 - *Why is sexual purity so important?*   24

Chapter 5 - *Sex: God's way or the world's way?*   29

Chapter 6 - *Valentine's Holiday to Spain: When honouring God became the most important thing to me*   34

Chapter 7 - *FAQ/ Questions that I am often asked*   37

Foreward

Before I even wrote a word of this book, I asked family members and friends whether I should write it. The reasons I was unsure included; would people really want to hear about my life? My Christian conversion? Would they want to hear the details (often uncomfortable) of my life? My admissions, thoughts, deepest secrets? Was it a secret vanity project? Did I just want praise and adoration? Was I trying to detract from Jesus and heap some sort of value upon myself?

The answer to all of the above is truly this; I want to glorify God. Our great, almighty, loving God who took my hard, stubborn, worldly, atheistic heart and changed it through the blood of His son, the Lord Jesus Christ. Praise be to my King.

Introduction

I wanted to write this book for a long time but was unsure where to begin and how to start. However, I knew that this was something God wanted me to do and was part of His plan for my life. I felt hopeful and optimistic when my confidence grew, and I decided to take that bold step in writing this book. As this is my first book, several ideas had been running through my mind and I wanted to make sure the message was clear and concise.

I wrote this book because I wanted to send a message out to young adults who may be finding it hard to prioritise God in their relationships or questioning whether it is a decision they should make. Hopefully, this book will encourage them to place God in their hearts and wholeheartedly follow His Word. God loves us and wants us to have a relationship with Him. There is a certain hope and peace in Jesus which He offers to all who come to Him.

Being in a Christian relationship has led me to discover so much about God's love and goodness, and I felt moved to write this and share with other young people in a similar age bubble. From my personal experience, I am confident and certain that God is worth suffering and living our lives for.

Love, God & Relationships explores the reasons why it is important to put God first in your life and the different ways you are able to honour Him. There is an ideal picture of what a Christian relationship should look like according to the Bible and God's Word. Furthermore, it elucidates how, and why, it varies from non-Christian relationships. This book encapsulates how living for God is not always easy but there are reasons why it is worth it.

Many Bible verses are used within this book as a guide for Christian living. They also demonstrate how one can focus one's mind and heart on Jesus each day. There are explanations with each verse to give further detail about what they mean for us today and how we can apply them to our lives. It is quintessential for them to be used as they illustrate what God says about love and relationships.

I expect this book to be used as a helpful tool for young people who are curious about what God and the Bible have to say about dating. This book should provide a bigger picture of the plan God has for their lives.

From this book, I hope that young adults see why living God's way is the best way and share this with others whom they know are finding it difficult or tricky to understand. I pray that from doing this, they will set a good and leading example which encourages and inspires others to live a life glorifying God.

Chapter 1
What does a Christian relationship look like?

When I first started dating my boyfriend, I was confused about how I would put God first in our relationship and what that would look like. As we were both Christians, we knew how important it was to honour God and take all our worries and fears to Him in prayer. Feeling slightly worried and unsure, I decided to ask my friend from my local church for some advice. She willingly pointed me to the Bible and talked through specific verses which were relevant to me.

To be completely honest, the Bible does not mention an awful lot about dating as the concept did not really exist back then. However, God does provide some principles for us to follow before entering marriage. This is helpful because it can encourage and equip us in glorifying God in our relationships.

2 Corinthians 6:14-15
'Do not be unequally yoked with unbelievers.

For what partnership has righteousness with lawlessness? Or what fellowship has light with darkness?'

Firstly, Paul makes it clear that it is not an option for a Christian to marry an unbeliever as this would lead us to make compromises in our beliefs and morals as well as debilitate our relationship with Christ. This clearly would not be helpful for a believer trying to develop a Christ-like relationship.

He uses contrasts such as light and dark to express how the couple would be working against each other rather than in harmony with one another. As he states, 'Do not', it shows how this is something which should be avoided and steered clear of as it will not help in our walk with God.

Considering this, Paul underlines how imperative it is to place God at the centre by having an intimate relationship with another believer. This is an ideal picture of a Christian relationship which will not hinder your walk with Christ but strengthen and encourage you in your faith.

> *1 Corinthians 6:18-19*
> *'Flee from sexual immorality. All other sins a person commits are outside the body, but whoever sins sexually, sins against their own body. Don't you know that your bodies are temples of the holy spirit, who is in you, whom you have received from God?'*

Paul uses the term 'sexual immorality' which is basically an umbrella term for any sexual acts outside of marriage. This includes: premarital sex, adultery, fornication, lust etc. He warns us to flee from this as we were not called by God to be impure, but to live a holy life (1 Thessalonians 4:7). This is important as God wants us to glorify Him in every way and not be hindered by worldly things.

1 Thessalonians 4:4-5
'Each of you should learn to control your own body in a way that is holy and honourable, not in passionate lust like the pagans who do not know God.'

God's way of dating and sex is completely opposite to the secular worldview and they clash with one another. God wants us to control our bodies and use them to glorify Him. The notion that it is acceptable for us to date around as much as we desire does not fit with God's plan and what he intended for us (1 Corinthians 10:23).

1 Corinthians 7:34
'An unmarried woman or virgin is concerned about the Lord's affairs: her aim is to be devoted to the Lord in both body and spirit.'

Here, Paul explains how essential it is for an unmarried Christian woman to love and prioritise the

Lord above all other things. He uses the word 'devoted' which means to be extremely loving and loyal.

For us to place one person in our hearts and say that they mean the most to us, would be idolatry. God is completely against this sin as it takes the glory away from Him and leads one to focus on oneself rather than the Creator.

> *Colossians 3:5*
> *'Put to death, therefore, whatever belongs to your earthly nature: sexual immorality, impurity, lust, evil desires and greed, which is idolatry.'*

Pray

Take some time to pray that you would put God first in your relationships and stand firm when trusting in Him. Ask for God's help to build your faith and guide you during times you feel down. Say sorry to God for times when you sin and make mistakes. Trust in His forgiveness and redemption of sins. Remember to thank Him for: His unending grace, the gift of the holy spirit, and His unconditional love for you.

Chapter 2
Your relationship with God

Our relationship with God should be at the forefront of our hearts and mind as it is important to have our quiet time with Him. However, things can pop up unexpectedly meaning we can't fit it in. Or we have had a bad day and do not feel in the right, or best, mood for it. Furthermore, our emotions can change each day, or our faith weakens. Whatever the reason may be, God's thoughts for us are of good and never of evil (Jeremiah 29:11). And we know that, in all things, God works for the good of those who love Him, who have been called according to His purpose (Romans 8:28).

It is important to remember that God does not keep a scoreboard of how many times you had quiet time, prayed or went to church as it is not to do with our works but with our faith in Him. 'But if it is by grace, it is no longer on the basis of works, otherwise grace is no longer grace' (Romans 11:6). However, we should always note these actions are a part of us trusting and depending our lives on Jesus and should be something that we willingly want to do because of Him giving Himself up on the cross.

Sometimes it may feel like God is distant and does not see or know what we are going through in our lives. With every trouble, trial or temptation we face, God is always walking with us, even when we feel like He is not, and He always has our best interests at heart.

> *1 Corinthians 15:22*
> *But Christ has indeed been raised*
> *from the dead… so in Christ all*
> *will be made alive.'*

It is unfortunate that many people do not care or realise that Jesus blessed us with a wonderful gift which should change our lives and the way we think about the world and perceive it - the chance to spend eternity in heaven with Him. 'For it is by grace you have been saved through faith- and this is not from yourselves, it is the gift of God' (Ephesians 2:8), 'therefore, there is now no condemnation for those who are in Christ Jesus' (Romans 8:1).

Because God has given us the gift of eternal life in Christ and made us a new creation, we are to live our lives for Him and keep His Word embedded in our hearts. 'For none of us lives for ourselves alone, and none of us dies for ourselves alone. If we live, we live for the Lord; and if we die, we die for the Lord' (Romans 14:7); 'And he died for all, that those who live should no longer live for themselves but for him who died for them and raised them again' (2 Corinthians 5:15).

> *Romans 8:18*
> *'I consider that our present*
> *sufferings are not worth*
> *comparing to the glory that*
> *will be revealed in us.'*

Many people think that there is no way to gain salvation just by accepting Jesus as your personal Lord and Saviour, and that it is too good to be true or there must be a catch somewhere. However, having a relationship with God is quite easy and not as difficult as many people think. Immediately we become children of God, we receive the Holy Spirit who will begin to guide and work in us. If you love me, keep my commands. 'And I will ask the Father, and He will give you another advocate to help you and be with you for ever - the Spirit of truth' (John 14:15).

Sin is what separated us from God from the beginning in the Garden of Eden and still does today. It creates problems in our relationship with Him. As Christians, we should not stop to think how much we can sin and still be classed as Christian but rather keep away from sin in the future and focus on pleasing God.

Sin creates the illusion that we can handle life ourselves without Jesus but only serves to draw us away from His love and peace. Thankfully, God has removed our transgressions from us and forgotten them, 'As far as the east is from the west, that is how far you have removed our transgressions from us' (Psalm 103:12). We should note that God is omniscient and Him forgetting is not the same as Him not remembering. God knows everything and forgets nothing but chooses to not remember our sins and wipes them away. He is always willing to give us chances and a fresh start to be made anew.

John 14:21
'The one who loves me will be loved by my Father. And I too will love them and show myself to them.'

Pray

Thank God that there is now no condemnation for us as He has blessed us with His perfect gift. Trust in the Holy Spirit to lead you away from sin and into God's love and grace. Thank God for always watching over us and having our best interests at heart. Pray that you would place your relationship with God at the centre of your heart.

Chapter 3
Why putting God first in your life and relationship is worth it

There are days when I question whether it is worth suffering for Christ as I try to live my life out for Him each day. Although it is hard to honour God during bad days and some can be easier than others, I always try to think of the positives and remember how blessed I am. I tend to wonder if the changes I make in my decisions show I am focused in following God and pleasing Him.

It can be easy to get distracted by challenges, issues and worries that life can bring. This can make us ask ourselves if God is really there and walking with us in our troubles and trials. We can have confidence in believing that God is always by our side and will never leave us nor forsake us (Deuteronomy 31:6).

It always reassures me to know that there are Bible verses about this which show that it is worth suffering for Christ and making the changes in our daily lives.

1 Corinthians 9:24
'Do you not know that in a race all the runners run, but only one gets the prize? Run in such a way as to get the prize. Everyone who competes in the games goes into strict training. They do it to get a crown that will not last; but we do it to get a crown that will last for ever.'

As Christians, we are enduring the suffering through the race and straining so that when we eventually get to the end, we will receive a prize for all our hard work.

One of Satan's schemes is to make us think it is pointless doing this as there is no healing or restoration which comes from it. The enemy tries to evoke the feeling of guilt and fear, so we do not reach the end of the race as we stop trusting God. His plans remain only to make us feel unworthy of God's forgiveness and lead us astray. As believers, we must remind ourselves that grace can always be received no matter what position we are in the race.

Paul says we should run the race and not stop to consider any alternatives or fall into sin which so easily entangles us but follow Jesus wholeheartedly with everything we have. The prize we will receive will eternally remain with us compared to the other runners who are struggling for a crown which will not last. He also mentions how this reward is completely worth the suffering.

> *1 Peter 1:8-9*
> *'Though you have not seen him,*
> *you love him; and even though*
> *you do not see him now, you*
> *believe in him and are filled*
> *with an inexpressible and*
> *glorious joy, for you are receiving*
> *the end result of your faith,*
> *the salvation of your souls.'*

It is worth following God as we receive a great amount of happiness. By having placing God's love indelibly in our hearts and putting our trust in Him, we become filled with peace and endless joy.

However, Satan tries to make persistent attempts to lure us away from the reality of our salvation even when we are aware of God's promises. He is fully aware of his eternal destiny in the lake of fire (Revelation 20:10) and so, serves only to steal, kill and destroy (John 10:10). He plants the lie into our mind that we are not really forgiven because he hates to see people come to Jesus and receive deliverance. The strikes of deception that the devil throws inevitably make it difficult for a believer to feel assured in God's love and faithfulness.

Peter states that we will undoubtedly gain salvation as the end result of our faith. He explains this as something we should look forward to and hope to enjoy. Because of this, we should not give up meeting with each other and spurring on one another in the faith (Hebrews 10:24). This can encourage us to stand firm and rest in God's abounding love for us.

Matthew 5:10
'Blessed are those who are

> *persecuted because of*
> *righteousness, for theirs*
> *is the kingdom of heaven.'*

> *Ephesians 2:8*
> *'For it is by grace you have*
> *been saved through faith-*
> *and this is not from yourselves,*
> *it is the gift of God.'*

God offers the gift of salvation to those who are ready to receive Christ as their personal saviour. This shows how putting God first is worth it because He gives us an eternal gift - for free! He loves us and wants us to be in a relationship with Him in faith and love.

> *1 Corinthians 15:58*
> *'Stand firm. Let nothing move*
> *you. Always give yourselves fully*
> *to the work of the Lord, because*
> *you know that your labour in the*
> *Lord is not in vain.'*

Pray

Thank God for the gift of salvation which is freely given to us as believers. Ask God for strength to resist the enemy's attacks and help us to rest in God's promises and love. Pray that you grow confident and certain of our eternal hope and peace. Be confident as you follow Jesus and trust Him with all your heart and mind. Pray that you would not stop running the race but receive joy and peace from God as you patiently wait for the end prize.

Chapter 4
Why is sexual purity so important?

Before I left home and moved out for university, I never really understood what it meant to be sexually pure and why it was important.

Occasionally, sex education had been taught at my all-girls secondary school and we learnt about staying safe sexually. The main message was to always use protection and only do what you feel comfortable with. As long as it felt right and you gave it a thumbs-up, there was no problem doing what you wanted, how you wanted.

We were taught that using protection such as condoms was the only way to be sexually safe and fully protected. This led me to wonder if sexual purity was something we remained in control of, as it had nothing to do with God. Moreover, I had never heard the subject being told from a biblical perspective or a Godly point of view.

Having accepted Jesus into my life, I have come to know of His grace and love. His plan for us to be sanctified (become more and more Christlike), and made holy, are reasons why we should avoid sexual immorality and keep ourselves pure.

> *2 Corinthians 5:17-21*
> *'Therefore, if anyone is in Christ,*
> *the new creation has come. The*
> *old is gone, the new is here!'*

This passage illustrates how our old natures have died, along with all their impurities, including sexual sin and we now live by faith, for the Creator who died for us. An analogy, for example, would be Jesus taking our filthy clothing and replacing it with brand new, clean garments.

Succinctly, Paul states we should reflect Jesus in our lives by living holy, sexually pure and sensible lives. If we profess to know Christ, we should not debate whether to control our lusts or give in to temptation but possess the fruits of the spirit unguardedly.

> *Ephesians 5:3*
> *'But among you there must not even be a hint of sexual immorality, or any kind of impurity, or of greed, because these are improper for God's holy people.'*

It is not ideal for Christians to have even a hint of sexual impurity or greed as these are not the qualities for a follower of Jesus. Moreover, it would not be possible to retain a healthy relationship with God. Paul stresses how it is important for God's holy people to stand out and show that they have Jesus in their lives.

Furthermore, Christ has identified us as His own by placing the Holy Spirit in our hearts which means we should not remain in unrepentant immorality but glorify God with our bodies.

> *1 Corinthians 10:23*
> *'I have the right to do anything' you say- but not everything is beneficial.*

I have the right to do anything- but not everything is constructive.'

Regarding relationships, one of Satan's tactics is to convince people to act based on feelings, which can change, instead of trusting in God, who does not change. He wants us to become the god of ourselves and encourage opposition to the kingdom of God. He is a deceiver, tempter and manipulator whose plan is to do everything he can to oppose God and those who follow Him.

Biblically speaking, Paul is stating that, as Christians, we should be set apart from the world, even in our relationships, and honour God in every aspect of our lives.

Thinking Time

How do these Bible verses show why purity and being sexually pure is important?

1 Timothy 4:12
'Don't let anyone look down on you because you

*are young, but set an example for the believers in speech,
in conduct, in love, in faith and in purity.'*

*Titus 2:5
'To be self-controlled, pure, working at home, kind and submissive to their own husbands, that the word of God may not be reviled.'*

*Matthew 5:5-8
'Blessed are the merciful, for they shall receive mercy. Blessed are the pure in heart for they shall see God.'*

Pray

Thank God for washing away all our sins and making us new creations in Christ. Ask Him to help you become more Christlike each day. Pray that others would see the fruits of the Spirit in you and the reflection of Jesus in your life. Trust Him to show you His compassion and grace as well as His Word. Believe in His promises of hope.

Chapter 5
Sex: God's way or the world's way?

Sex is something that is a big part of our society. It is something that is not really talked about but is something we cannot escape when most songs, movies are all about it. Society says that our sexuality is our choice, how we feel and what we make it to be. The world says that sexuality is down to your personal choice and has lowered its significance greatly. God's view of sex is in complete opposition to this, and the views seem to contradict and clash with one another.

Here are some Bible verses to show what God says about sex and how we are to live our lives for Him:

> *Romans 13:13-14*
> *'Let us behave decently, as in the daytime, not in carousing and drunkenness, not in sexual immorality and debauchery, not in dissension*
> *and jealousy. Rather, clothe yourselves with the Lord Jesus*

> *Christ, and do not think about*
> *how to gratify the desires of the flesh.'*

As Christians, we should behave sensibly and reflect Jesus in our actions and decisions. We should not participate in sexual sin which draws us further away from our Heavenly Father.

Rather than walk in the spirit, sexual sin only serves to gratify fleshly desires. The devil perverts God's creation of sex by twisting His Word just as he did in the Garden of Eden when he said, 'Did God really say that?' This is present in today's society where the authority of God continues to be challenged and rebelled against. When we give in to temptation not of God and allow it to make its way into our hearts, lust begins to dominate our actions and lead us into the direction distant from God.

When a couple have sex outside of marriage, they indulge in pleasures not meant for them and they take sex outside of the context which God designed. By using sexuality to solely satisfy fleshly lusts, we devalue the powerful gift God has given us and its beauty becomes cheapened. We cannot experience the Holy Spirit if we carry on in unrepentant sexual sin. As with any sin, there are consequences for going against God's words.

> *Genesis 2:24*
> *'Therefore, a man shall leave his father and*
> *his mother and hold*
> *fast to his wife, and they shall*
> *become one flesh.'*

Some people think that God is opposed to pleasure, but He is not. Sex was God's idea and He created it as a gift for us to enjoy within the bounds of marriage.

God said it was 'very good' when He brought the first man, Adam to Eve and joined them together in marriage. He designed sex within the confines of a committed marital relationship and since He created it, He has every right to set the boundaries for it. God commands complete abstinence before marriage and declares anything outside of this context to be sinful (Acts 15:20, Galatians 5:19, Colossians 3:5, Ephesians 5:3, Jude 7, 1 Thessalonians 4:3). God advises us to wait until marriage because it honours Him, keeps us sexually safe and ensures that we do not get hurt emotionally.

> *Romans 12:2*
> *'Do not conform to the pattern of*
> *this world but be transformed by*
> *the renewing of your mind. Then*
> *you will be able to test and approve what*
> *God's will is--his good,*
> *pleasing and perfect will.'*

Satan wants us to submit to worldly ways and tries to tempt individuals in any way possible, including sexual sin and temptation. His aim is to divert our hearts from following God's laws concerning sex and become submissive to God's truth.

Most of the time, following the trend and joining in with the crowd can seem like the easier option, but it may not always be the best option.

As believers, we do not belong to this world and we should not conform to its pattern. For instance, it is like the world is dancing to the same song but as Christians we decide not to partake in the trend or pattern which everyone is following. We have a much greater purpose and are to set our minds on things above, not on earthly things (Colossians 3:2).

Sinning sexually also carries spiritual significance and does not merely defile just our physical bodies. It is a grave sin which is directly opposed to God's plan for us to experience his good, pleasing and perfect will.

Pray

Pray that you would honour God sexually and glorify Him with your body. Ask God to use the Holy Spirit to guide you. Remember to thank Him for his steadfast love and praise Him for His goodness.

Chapter 6
Valentine's Holiday to Spain: When honouring God became the most important thing to me

As this was my first serious relationship, I felt nervous and worried about dating my boyfriend and us being together. I tended to refuse going out to places because I was scared and not used to the whole dating concept. I decided that this needed to change in order for me to form a much healthier relationship that we would both grow and encourage one another in.

I had known my boyfriend for several months before we decided to travel together to Spain for Valentine's Day. He was a few years older than me and had been in more relationships in the past than I had.

We had asked for separate rooms in our hotel to make sure we had our own space and were not alone together so that we would not be drawn into temptation. When the hotel assistant offered an alternative and said it would be more cost effective for us to stay in one room, we both struggled to stick to what we knew was right and what God wanted us to do in that situation.

We had a viewing of the room and were rather pleased with it. It seemed as if there was nothing wrong; it was cheaper and a better deal than what we expected. But I thought,' we're not married, how can we sleep in the same bed? Does the Bible allow that? Is this right?' When I spoke up and clearly said 'This isn't right. I would still like the separate rooms please', everyone looked as if there was something wrong with me. That was when I knew that the spirit was truly at work in me, and it was God re-focusing my mind on glorifying and honouring him.

We enjoyed visiting the: Palaces, museums, cafes, gardens and other famous landmarks of Madrid. Sharing our interests and much more personal things became much easier as time went on, and we learned to appreciate being around one another and enjoying each other's presence.

When I saw that we had grown a lot together and felt comfortable around each other, it became harder to resist temptation and honour God because I felt like I knew him and could share anything that was on my mind.

To this day, I still believe relying and waiting patiently for God is always best, especially when you feel unsure or uncertain about things. I thanked God for His faithfulness and mercies upon my life as I knew He was the one who guided me through everything and showed me that His way is the best.

Chapter 7
FAQ/ Questions that I am often asked

It is common and normal for young adults to be unsure about feelings in a relationship and what they truly want. Emotions such as doubt, fear and worry can come into play, leaving them feeling less solid and grounded in their faith. This may also leave them with a number of thoughts and questions. You might feel alone but I can assure you that this is something any believer can experience. Here are some questions I get asked frequently.

What would be your no.1 tip to a young Christian couple trying to live for Jesus?

Trust Jesus and place Him first in your hearts to grow together and encourage one another in your faith. Praying is a great way to do this.

How strict were you on the no-sex rule when you first started your relationship?

I told my boyfriend I couldn't

continue with the relationship unless we stuck to it. I wanted to honour God and make sure that came first before anything else.

Did you like him from the start?
To be honest, I wasn't really sure how I felt about him. It took some time to get to know him more and see that I was interested in building a relationship.

Do you go to church/Christian events together?
Yes! We love doing this as we feel it encourages the both of us to serve the Lord and place him first in our hearts. This is definitely a great way to build a Christian relationship.

www.ingramcontent.com/pod-product-compliance
Lightning Source LLC
Chambersburg PA
CBHW071506080526
44587CB00016B/2716